STAGE 2

P9-DNX-357

Snakes Are Hunters

by Patricia Lauber

illustrated by Holly Keller

HarperCollinsPublishers

HarperCollins®, ☎®, and Let's-Read-and-Find-Out Science® are trademarks of HarperCollins Publishers Inc.

The Let's-Read-and-Find-Out Science book series was originated by Dr. Franklyn M. Branley, Astronomer Emeritus and former Chairman of the American Museum–Hayden Planetarium, and was formerly co-edited by him and Dr. Roma Gans, Professor Emeritus of Childhood Education, Teachers College, Columbia University. Text and illustrations for each of the books in the series are checked for accuracy by an expert in the relevant field. For more information about Let's-Read-and-Find-Out Science books, write to Harper-Collins Children's Books, 1350 Avenue of the Americas, New York, NY 10019, or visit our website at www.letsreadandfindout.com.

Library of Congress Cataloging-in-Publication Data
Lauber, Patricia.
   Snakes are hunters.
   (Let's-read-and-find-out science. Stage 2)
   Summary: Describes the physical characteristics of a variety of snakes and how they hunt, catch, and eat their prey.
   ISBN 0-690-04628-6 — ISBN 0-690-04630-8 (lib. bdg.) — ISBN 0-06-445091-0 (pbk.)
   1. Snakes—Juvenile literature. [1. Snakes] I. Keller, Holly, ill. II. Title. III. Series.
QL666.06L345 1988   87-47695
597.96

Snakes Are Hunters

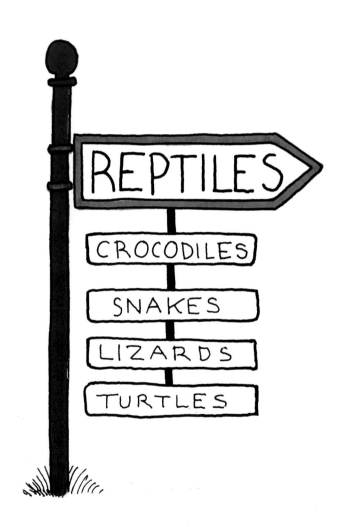

ANACONDA
FROM
SOUTH AMERICA

RETICULATE PYTHON
FROM
ASIA

ROCK PYTHON
FROM
AFRICA

YOUNG
EXPLORERS'
CLUB

If you want to see really big snakes, a zoo is the place to go. You will never find these snakes near your home. Big snakes come from jungles and other hot parts of the world.

5

ANACONDA

RED-BELLIED WATER SNAKE

BULL SNAKE

TIMBER RATTLESNAKE

GARTER SNAKE

BALL PYTHON

BLACK RAT SNAKE

KING COBRA

KING SNAKE

You will also see small snakes and middle-sized snakes. But no zoo can show you every kind. All together, there are more than 3,000 kinds of snakes.

CORN SNAKE

MILK SNAKE

A SNAKE'S BELLY SCALES ARE BIGGER THAN THE REST.

Look at some snakes and you will see ways they are all alike. Each has a long body that is covered with scales. The scales overlap like shingles on a roof.

Every snake has round eyes. The eyes never blink because a snake has no eyelids. Instead, each eye has a clear cover called a spectacle. The spectacle protects the eye.

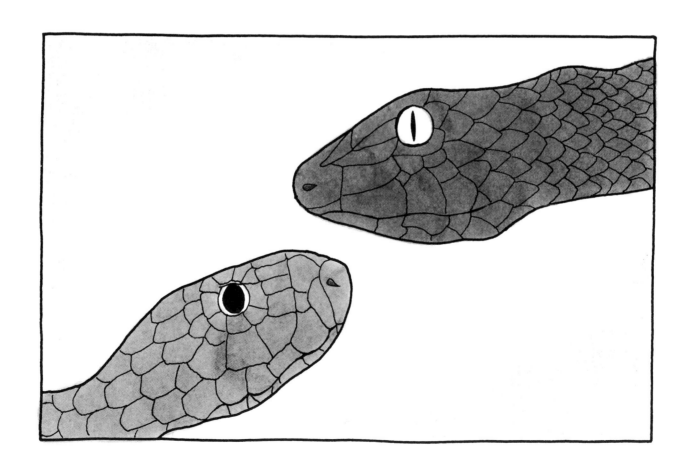

A snake has no legs. Even so, it gets around very well. Many snakes can glide over the ground, climb trees, and swim.

Snakes move in several ways. Most often you see one moving with S-shaped curves of its body. The curves push against rough spots on the ground, and the snake slides forward.

Snakes are hunters. In the wild they find and catch other animals for food.

This garter snake is hunting. It first senses that something is near when the frog hops. Snakes cannot hear sounds as we do. But they can sense the shaking of the ground when an animal hops or runs.

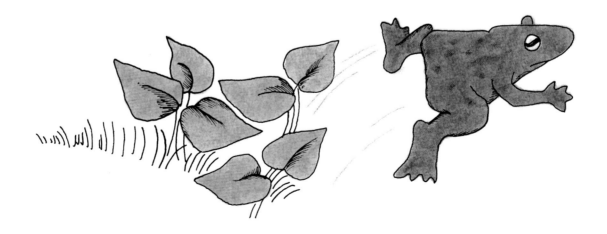

The garter snake looks around, watching for movement.
But mostly it hunts by scent. It uses its nostrils to scent
prey. It also uses the long, forked tongue that flicks in and
out of its mouth. The two tips of the tongue pick up tiny
particles of scent and carry them to the roof of the mouth.
There the particles are tasted and smelled.

The garter snake glides closer and closer to its prey.
It strikes, using its teeth to catch the frog.

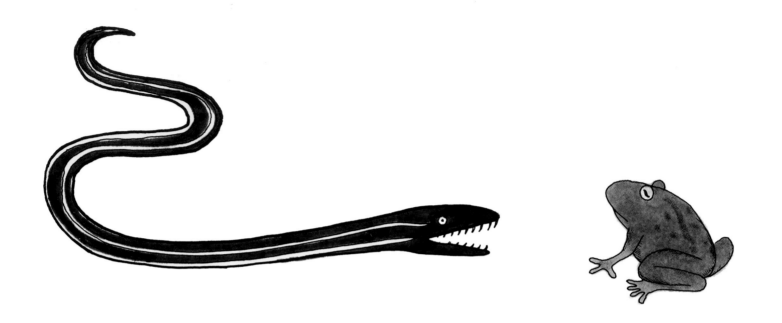

A snake's teeth are like curved needles. They are good for catching food but not for chewing. Snakes swallow their prey whole.

The frog is bigger than the garter snake's head. But the snake can swallow it anyway.

A snake's jaws open very wide. The lower jaw drops much farther than yours does. And it is made of two pieces of bone that stretch apart. Bones of the upper jaw also stretch apart.

A snake eats by moving bones in its jaws. Bit by bit, its teeth pull the meal into the snake's throat.

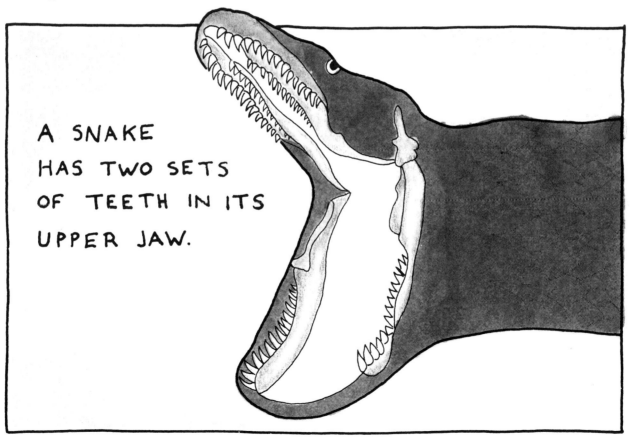

A SNAKE HAS TWO SETS OF TEETH IN ITS UPPER JAW.

The garter snake eats its prey live. Many snakes do this. But some kinds kill their prey before eating it. A corn snake kills by squeezing. This one has caught a mouse. The snake quickly wraps several coils of its body around the mouse. Each time the mouse breathes out, the coils tighten. Soon the mouse cannot breathe. It dies, and the corn snake starts to swallow it.

Boas, pythons, and anacondas also kill their prey this way. They usually feed on chickens or large rats. But these big snakes sometimes kill and swallow small deer or pigs. After such a huge meal, they may not need to eat again for several months.

A rattlesnake is one of the snakes that can sense heat. It has a hollow, or pit, on each side of its head. The pits sense tiny changes in air temperature. That is how a rattler knows when it is near a warm-blooded animal. A rattler can find its prey even in the dark.

The rattler is also one of the snakes that kill their prey with poison. Inside its mouth are two long teeth, called fangs. Each is hollow and is linked to a sac of poison, or venom. As the rattler strikes, venom is forced through the fangs. The prey dies and the rattler feeds.

WHEN THE RATTLER'S FANGS ARE NOT IN USE, THEY ARE FOLDED BACK IN THE MOUTH.

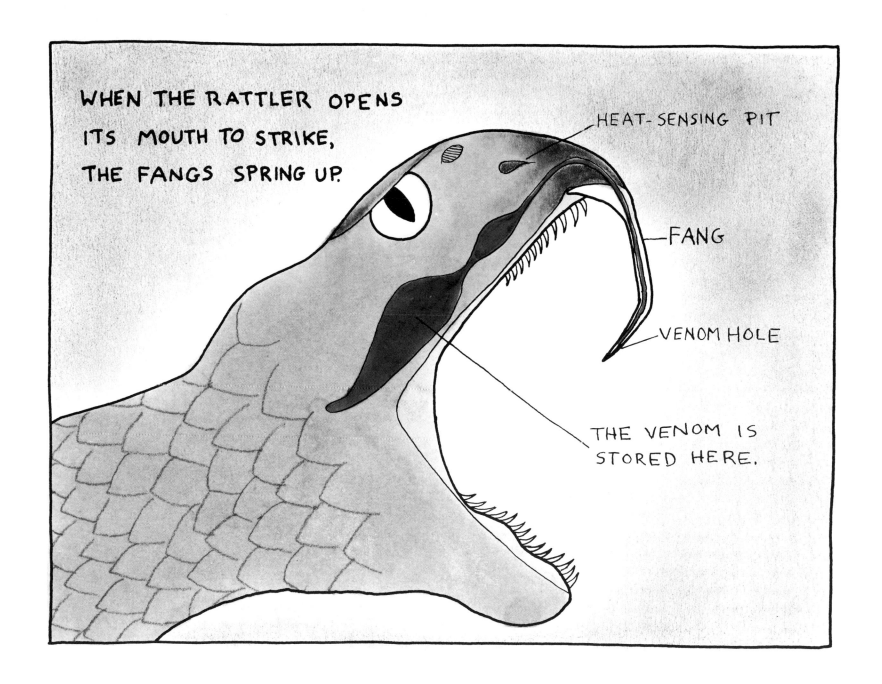

WHEN THE RATTLER OPENS ITS MOUTH TO STRIKE, THE FANGS SPRING UP.

HEAT-SENSING PIT

FANG

VENOM HOLE

THE VENOM IS STORED HERE.

Snakes often spend hours looking for food. Some hunt for it. Others wait for prey to pass by. But snakes do not always get a meal. The prey may escape or fight back.

Snakes are also hunted themselves. Young snakes, small snakes, and middle-sized snakes are food for many other animals. They are even eaten by other snakes. Sometimes big snakes get eaten too. They are hunted by crocodiles and other large animals.

Snakes need the sun's heat. A snake's body cannot make its own heat the way yours does. It needs to take heat from the sun or from sun-warmed rocks or water.

A snake's body cannot get rid of heat the way yours does, either. To cool off, a snake must find a cool place. Snakes die if they get too hot.

Many snakes live where winters are cold. They must find safe shelters for winter. Snakes die if temperatures are below freezing.

The snakes seek out deep burrows and caves. These are places where temperatures stay above freezing. Here hundreds of snakes may gather in autumn. They go into a long, deep sleep.

Snakes wake when the spring sun warms the air and ground. They sun themselves. They hunt. They look for mates.

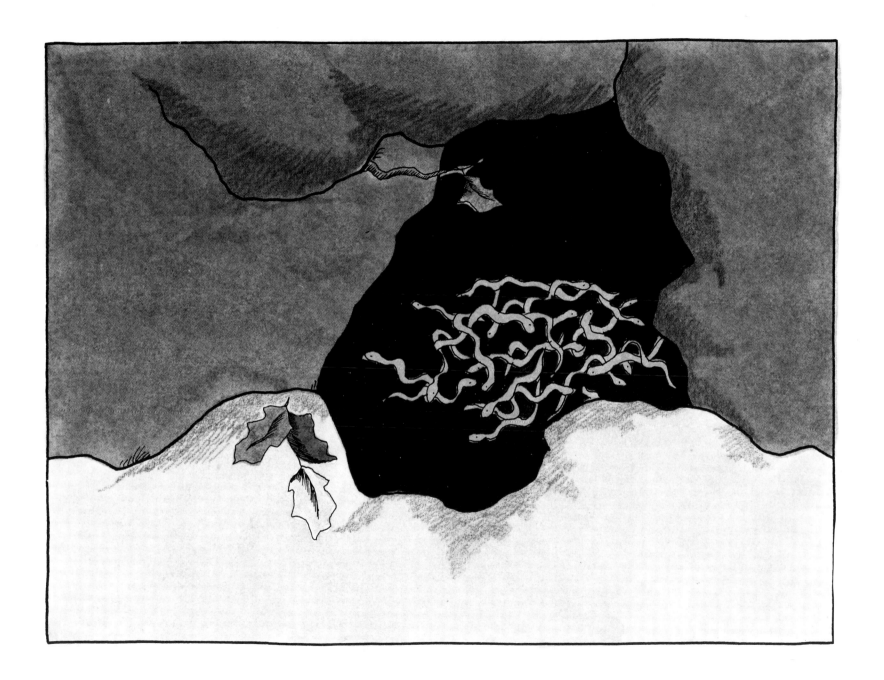

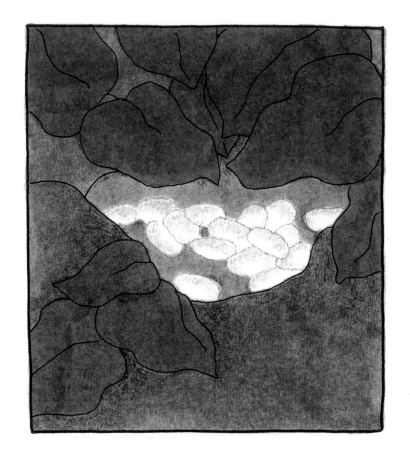

Many female snakes lay eggs. They make a nest in a warm, damp place, lay their eggs, and go away. The young hatch out by themselves. With some kinds of snakes, the eggs stay in the female's body until they hatch. The young are born live.

Young snakes can take care of themselves. Soon after birth or hatching, they are ready to hunt insects and other small animals.

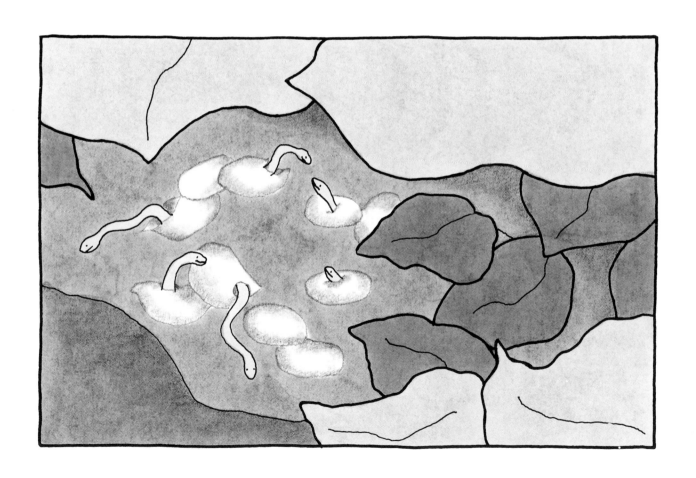

As a young snake grows, its thin outer skin becomes too tight. The snake must shed the skin. It rubs its head on something rough, loosening the old skin around the lips. As the snake goes on rubbing, the skin is peeled back from the head. The snake crawls out of the old skin, wearing a shiny new one. Now it can go on growing. It will shed its skin many times during its life.

A SNAKE'S OLD SKIN IS SO THIN YOU CAN ALMOST SEE THROUGH IT.

Big snakes may live to be 30 years old. Smaller snakes
may live to be 15 to 20 if nothing happens to them, but often
something does. Snakes are most likely to live a long time in
a zoo, the best place for you to see and watch them.

FIND OUT MORE ABOUT A GIANT SNAKE

The anaconda is the largest snake in the Americas and probably the world. It is a close relative of the boas and pythons. Some anacondas have measured more than thirty-three feet long. But most are no more than sixteen feet. They are more heavily built than pythons—most are more than a foot thick in the middle. Some weigh up to 550 pounds.

Anacondas spend much of their time in water. They live along slow-moving rivers, ponds, and swamps. Anacondas mate in or very near the water. After nine months, a female gives birth to anywhere from fourteen to eighty-two babies, each more than twenty-four inches in length. The young grow to be almost ten feet long by age three.

Anacondas do not chase their prey. They wait in the water for prey to come to drink—deer, sheep, pigs. An anaconda seizes a large animal by the neck and instantly throws its coils around the animal's body. Each time the prey breathes out, the coils tighten. Soon the prey can no longer breathe. After a big meal, the snake may not need to eat again for two or three months.